The Irish

Greg Nickles

CRABTREE
Publishing Company
www.crabtreebooks.com

CRABTREE
Publishing Company

PMB 16A, 350 Fifth Avenue
Suite 3308
New York, NY 10118

612 Welland Avenue
St. Catharines, Ontario
L2M 5V6

Co-ordinating editor: Ellen Rodger
Production co-ordinator: Rosie Gowsell
Assistant editor: Lisa Gurusinghe

Prepress: Embassy Graphics
Printer: Worzalla Publishing Company

Created by: Brown Partworks Ltd
Commissioning editor: Anne O'Daly
Project editor: Clare Oliver
Picture researcher: Adrian Bentley
Designer: Abdul Rafique
Maps: Mark Walker
Consultant: Professor Donald Avery Ph.D, History

CATALOGING-IN-PUBLICATION DATA
Nickles, Greg, 1969-
    The Irish / Greg Nickles.
    p.cm. – (We came to North America)
    Includes index.
    ISBN 0-7787-0190-5 (RLB) – ISBN 0-7787-0204-9
(pbk.)
    1. Irish Americans–History–Juvenile literature. 2.
Irish Americans–Biography–Juvenile literature. 3. Irish
Americans–Social life and customs–Juvenile literature
[1. Irish Americans–History]   I. Title II. Series
    E184.I6 N53 2001
    973'.049162–dc21
                    00-069363
                    LC

Photographs
AKG London Trinity College, Dublin 6 (top);
The Art Archive Sheffield City Art Galleries 11
(bottom left); Brown Partworks Library of
Congress 7, 11 (bottom right), 16, 24, 25 (bottom)
31 (top); National Archives 4 (top), 30 (top);
Corbis 9 (top); Bettmann 31 (bottom);
Jan Butchofsky-Houser 5; Francine Fleischer 31
(top); Mike Zens 4 (bottom); Sandy Felsenthal 26
(bottom); Ted Spiegel 8 Glenbow Archives,
Calgary, Canada (NA-3022-1) 27 (top);
(NA-2025-2) 27 (bottom); Hulton Getty 15 (top),
15 (bottom), 19; Sean Sexton 10; Image Bank,
Andrea Pistolesi 23; Archive Photos 26 (top);
Mary Evans Picture Library 14 (top); National
Archives of Canada (C-8482) 30 bottom; North
Wind Picture Archives title page, 9 (bottom), 11
(top), 14 (bottom), 17 (bottom), 20, 25 (top), 28
(bottom); Parks Canada, Helene Boucher 17 (top);
Peter Newark's Pictures 13, 21 (bottom left), 21
(bottom right); Ronald Grant Archive 29;
Skyscan Kevin Dwyer 6 (bottom); TRIP,
Spencer Grant 28 (top).

Cover: A young fiddler at an Irish traditional
music festival. The fiddle is an important
instrument in Irish music.

Book Credits
page 12: From the Cork Evening Post,
March 31, 1847.
pages 18 and 22: Library of Congress, Manuscript
Division, WPA Federal Writers' Project Collection.

Contents

Introduction

Many millions of people in the United States and Canada share Irish **ancestors** and celebrate Irish holidays, festivals, and heroes. The people of Ireland brought their traditions, religions and beliefs to North America where they helped build and define their nations.

Irish **immigrants** were some of the first Europeans to settle in North America, in the early 1600s. Millions more arrived in the 1700s, 1800s, and 1900s. Their journey was often a dangerous one that took them across the stormy Atlantic Ocean in crowded sailing ships.

Most of the immigrants had little choice but to leave Ireland. Some fled unemployment, ruthless landlords, and conflicts with the ruling British government. The Great **Famine** (1845-1849) and other crop failures brought mass starvation and disease that forced millions more to **emigrate**.

▲ These Irish immigrants to Boston in the 1880s found work digging clams.

▼ Irish Americans celebrate their heritage on St. Patrick's Day.

Christian Conflicts

Since the 1500s, differences in religion have caused many conflicts in Ireland and Europe. Both Roman Catholic and Protestant Churches are **denominations** of **Christianity**. The Roman Catholic Church is led by the **Pope**, who lives in the Vatican in Rome. Protestant Churches, which first formed in the 1500s, split away from the Roman Catholic Church because they believed the Pope and his church were **corrupt**. In the following centuries, Christians of both denominations often waged war on one another. When they moved to North America, they brought with them mistrust of one another.

▼ This statue on Ellis Island commemorates Annie Moore and her brothers. She was the first of over a million Irish who arrived in New York during the famine.

Some Irish immigrants had money, job skills, and spoke English, which helped them quickly succeed in their new land. They found steady work and won the respect of their communities. Irish **Protestants** were especially welcomed in North America, where most people involved in government and business also belonged to Protestant churches.

For other Irish, success was harder to find. They came to North America penniless, hungry, and without the skills needed for decent work. Many also spoke Irish as their first language. These people struggled to escape poverty and earn respect. Irish **Roman Catholics** had to work especially hard to fight **prejudice** from the Protestants, but they played a key role in establishing the Roman Catholic Church in North America, especially in the United States. The church also provided a source of education and social life.

By the end of the twentieth century, **descendants** of the Irish had spread westward across North America. They helped build farms, towns, factories, and railroads, and served in all levels of business, government, and the military.

A Long History

North America's Irish communities share a passionate love for their island homeland, which is called "Eire" in the Irish language. Ireland earned another name, the "Emerald Isle," from its vast, rolling pastures of lush, green grass.

However beautiful the land, Ireland's people have suffered wars and other hardships over the centuries. Some of their most recent and painful struggles have been against their neighbor Great Britain.

The history of Ireland stretches back many thousands of years. The first recorded people there were the Celts, sometimes called Gaels, who lived there about 2,000 years ago. They divided the land between them into several kingdoms. The kings ruled over the nobles, who owned the land, and the peasants who farmed it. The Celts spoke a language called Gaelic, which spread over Ireland.

In about 400 A.D., Roman Catholic **missionaries** arrived to **convert** the Irish. Within decades, the people accepted Christianity, and Ireland became a famous center of worship.

▲ The religious *Book of Kells* was beautifully illustrated at Kells, near Dublin, by **medieval** Irish monks.

◄ These stone figures stand near an ancient cemetery on Boa Island in County Fermanagh, Ireland. They are called the Janus statues and are around 2,000 years old.

Ireland's Patron Saint

St. Patrick is a saint celebrated by the Roman Catholic Church. He is also a symbol of Ireland and one of its heroes. Although little is known about his life, it is believed that around 400 A.D., a boy named Patrick was captured, sent to Ireland, and was forced into slavery. Several years later he escaped and joined the Church. After an inspiring dream, he returned to Ireland to bring Christianity to its people. Of his many **feats**, it is claimed that he converted the Irish, ordained priests, and founded churches. Patrick made the **shamrock** a famous Irish symbol.

▲ Not only English and Scots settled in Ireland. French Protestants called Huguenots, moved there to work as weavers in the 1600s. As a result, Belfast became an important center for producing linen.

In 1171, Ireland was conquered by the English king, Henry II. Over the next 400 years, the Irish rose many times against their British rulers, but never won back control of their country. Bitter feelings increased after England and Scotland adopted Protestantism in the 1500s. The Irish remained Roman Catholics. The Protestants used their dislike of the Catholic faith as reason to treat the Irish harshly.

In the centuries following, Britain tightened its hold on Ireland. Irish landowners were replaced with Protestants loyal to the British. English and Scottish settlers took over Ireland's fertile region of Ulster, and formed the Plantation of Ulster in 1609. The Penal Laws passed by the Protestant Irish government of the 1600s and 1700s, banned Irish Roman Catholics from worshiping freely, voting, owning land, and teaching.

Many Irish were peasants because they were not allowed to own land. Renting land from British colonists, they had no money or power. The Irish peasants grew grain and raised livestock to sell to the British market in order to pay rent. They depended on potatoes for their own food.

▼ Ireland lies to the west of Great Britain. From the 1600s, English and Scottish Protestants crossed the Irish Sea to take over the land in Ulster in the north of the country.

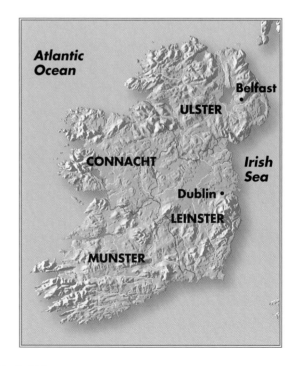

The First Irish Immigrants

The Irish were among the first European settlers to come to North America, in the early 1600s. Over the next 200 years, they settled throughout Britain's colonies, which stretched down the east coast of the continent.

These **colonies** included the thirteen that became the first United States in 1776, as well as Newfoundland, New Brunswick, and Nova Scotia in Canada.

Life was difficult for the settlers in the 1600s. Some settlers died for lack of food and supplies, others died from the bitter weather or from disease. Battles with local Native peoples, from whom the settlers had taken the land, also claimed many lives.

By the 1700s, the colonies were better established. Coastal cities, especially New York, had grown into busy centers of trade. Many jobs became available, as opposed to the farm work, **trapping**, fishing, and **logging** of the century before.

During this period, people arrived from all groups of Irish society. Many were the descendants of Scots who had once settled in Northern Ireland. They became known as the "Scotch Irish" because of their **heritage**.

▶ Few Irish immigrants were as successful as John Barry (175-1803). He is considered the father of the U.S. Navy and won many victories in the War of Independence (1775–1783).

Many thousands of Irish immigrants of the 1600s and 1700s, including the Scotch Irish, came from Protestant families and had money and an education, or a skilled trade. Some wanted the freedom to worship as they saw fit. Most of these settlers found success in their new home.

Not all Irish immigrants of this period came from such privileged backgrounds. Thousands of peasants could not pay for their voyage across the Atlantic. To cover their costs, they became **indentured servants** to wealthy North American colonists. After working for several years, these servants were freed and allowed to start new lives. Some people served their term and went on to become successful. Others did not survive the harsh work conditions of their service.

▲ During the 1600s, there were armed battles between Native peoples and the European colonists.

▼ Life was tough, even for the Irish who were able to find land and build a home.

No Choice

Not everyone had the choice to move to the New World. In addition to allowing thousands of willing Irish immigrants to leave, the British also forced many Irish prisoners and homeless people to work in its colonies. For most of them, sent to miserable jobs in mines and on **plantations**, the trip to North America meant a harsh life from overwork, accidents on the job, and **malnourishment**.

The Great Famine

Ireland faced even greater hardships in the 1800s than in previous centuries. More people than ever before left for other lands.

The population of Ireland grew quickly in the 1800s, but there were not enough jobs for everyone. Many Irish Catholics were unable to feed, house, and clothe themselves. They lived in poverty, in homes that often were no more than huts. By the end of the century, Ireland had lost half its population to starvation and disease or emigration.

As the prices for the transatlantic trip dropped and cheap or free North American land became accessible, more people emigrated to look for work. Famines, caused by crop failures in the late 1700s and early 1800s, forced others to leave.

In 1845, disaster struck Ireland. A fungus called blight infected the potato crops, turning the potatoes into black mush. The blight continued until 1850. Without their main food, millions of people faced starvation. This terrible period in Ireland's history is known as the Great Famine.

▲ When people could not pay their rent, they were evicted, or forced out of their homes. The police used forced entry into tenant houses to throw out the poor families living there.

Suffering Ignored

The horrible suffering throughout Ireland during the Great Famine was mostly ignored by the country's British rulers. The British government under Prime Minister Robert Peel did offer some meals to the starving and created jobs, in which the needy worked to earn money for food. This saved only a few thousand lives, and left millions of Irish in misery. The heartless neglect of the government during the Great Famine is remembered by people around the world as one of the greatest crimes of the nineteenth century.

▲ **Impoverished Irish peasants work the land in County Mayo, Ireland.**

More than a million Irish died during the Great Famine. They died from starvation, and diseases, such as typhus, cholera, dysentery, and smallpox, which spread quickly among those weakened by hunger. They died while some farms continued to grow grain and raise meat. These foods were not fed to the hungry people. Desperate to pay their rent to avoid being evicted, farmers sold their crops instead to Britain.

Fleeing hunger and disease, over a million impoverished Irish left their island. Even after the Famine they continued to leave, tempted by stories of plentiful food and work. By the early 1900s, over two million more had emigrated, most bound for North America.

▲ **This magazine cover of the 1880s shows a starving Irish woman waving a "Help" sign to American ships. There is a subtle suggestion of death in the background.**

◄ **During the 1800s many Irish lived in miserable cabins. Large families slept, ate, and lived in just one room.**

Eyewitness to History

ELIHU BARRIT was an American who visited Ireland for a week in February 1847, during the Great Famine. He wrote to Massachusetts's *Christian Citizen* to describe the suffering he saw there, in the hope that more Americans would contribute to the Irish relief fund.

" As soon as we opened the door, a crowd of haggard creatures pressed upon us, and with agonizing prayers for bread, followed us to the soup kitchen. One poor woman, whose cries became irresistably **importunate**, had watched all day in the graveyard, lest the body of her husband be stolen from its last resting place, to which he had been **consigned** yesterday. She had five children sick with famine fever in her hovel, and she raised an exceedingly bitter cry for help.

We entered the graveyard, in the midst of which was a small watch house. This miserable shed had served as a grave where the dying could bury themselves. It was seven feet long and six in breadth… And into this noisome **sepulcher** diving men, women and children went down to die; to pillow upon the rotten straw, the grave clothes vacated by **preceding** victims, and festering with their fever. Here they lay as closely to each other as if crowded side by side on the bottom of one grave. Six persons had been found in this fetid sepulcher at one time, and with only one able to crawl to the door and to ask for water. Removing a board from the entrance of this black hole of **pestilence**, we found it crammed with **wan** victims of famine, ready and willing to perish. A quiet, **listless** despair broods over the population, and cradles men for the grave. "

The Journey

During the years of the Great Famine, the journey of the Irish to North America was often worse than the starvation they left at home.

Crossing the ocean in wooden sailing ships had always been risky, but ships in Famine times were filthy, overcrowded, and infested with disease. So many thousands of people died aboard these vessels that they became known as "coffin ships."

Previous Irish emigrants often could afford transportation on decent ships designed to carry passengers. The hundreds of thousands of impoverished Irish who left during the Famine, boarded any ship that would take them. On the first part of their journey to the English port of Liverpool, passengers were often crammed onto crude **freight ships** together with livestock or coal.

Transatlantic ships left from Liverpool for North America. Shipping companies and captains, eager to make money from the surge of passengers, used every ship they could find to carry the Irish. All types of vessels, from the old small unseaworthy to brand-new, were pressed into service. There were not enough skilled men to sail the ships, so they sailed with inexperienced crews. Passengers were packed aboard by the hundreds.

The many dangers that faced the Irish on the five-to-six-week journey included shipboard fires, raging storms, and jagged ocean reefs. Many ships sank, taking with them all aboard. The unskilled crews often made mistakes that led to such disasters. To make matters worse, some also mistreated the Irish, beating them, or locking them below decks for days or weeks at a time.

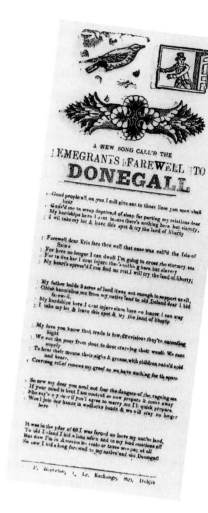

▲ **This songsheet of the 1850s shows a musical "goodbye" to Ireland.**

▶ **Passenger bunks on the ships were dirty, overcrowded, and often were infested with disease.**

Improving the Trip

In the years following the Famine, conditions on the ships gradually improved. Masts and sails were replaced by steam-powered engines that made ships much faster. By 1900, the transatlantic voyage was shortened to just a couple of weeks instead of double or triple that time. Ships made more frequent trips and carried fewer passengers, which led to less crowding and disease. Ships also needed fewer supplies for the trip, so people were better fed.

◄ **These third-class passengers of the 1930s celebrate nearing the Canadian coast by dancing on deck.**

▼ **Bound for Liverpool, then to North America, steamships are packed with people. Others wait on the docks for a place on another ship.**

Disease was by far the worst hazard. Infections spread below decks, where passengers crowded into unwashed bunks barely large enough to lie in. The risk increased as people grew weak from starvation and thirst. Ruthless captains, wanting to save money, rarely carried enough food and drink to supply all their passengers for the whole journey.

Stories of miserable and dangerous ocean trips made it back to Ireland. The Irish were so desperate to escape their hunger and poverty, that thousands continued to **embark**.

First Impressions

If they survived their ocean voyage, the Irish landed at the ports along North America's east coast. In the United States the main port of entry was New York, a young city that by the 1800s was already one of the world's largest. In Canada, Québec City was the key port of entry.

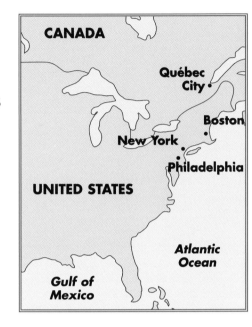

Even after their ships docked, the Irish were not guaranteed to set foot on shore. First, an inspector had to board their vessel and make sure they were healthy. If he saw evidence of disease, he put the passengers or even the entire ship under **quarantine**. Quarantined passengers were not allowed into the cities for fear of diseases being spread among the local people. With no modern medicines to stop illnesses, city officials were afraid of a city-wide **epidemic**.

Dishonest captains made the job of the inspectors more difficult by hiding evidence of the poor conditions on their ships. Hours before they entered port, the captains ordered passengers to clean out their quarters and scrub down decks that had not been washed in months. This trick made it harder to determine which ships should be quarantined.

▲ Ships carrying Irish immigrants landed at east-coast ports, such as New York, Boston, Philadelphia, and Québec City.

When a ship was quarantined, no one was allowed to leave or board, except for the doctors and their helpers, until everyone there had recovered.

▶ It could take a doctor hours to examine and question all the immigrants on a ship.

Grosse Île, Québec

Today, a monument stands on the island of Grosse Île, near the city of Québec, in Canada. It commemorates more than 5,400 Irish who fled to Canada in the summer of 1847, only to die soon after they arrived. Before immigrants entered Québec City at the time, the government made them stop at Grosse Île for inspection. The number of infected immigrants, and the death toll left many Irish children orphaned. In March 1848, Ignace Bourget, a French-Canadian Roman Catholic bishop of Montreal, asked the community to adopt Irish orphans. Many French-Canadians adopted orphans and allowed them to keep their Irish last names. Today, there are many French-Canadians who have Irish last names, such as Ryan, Johnson, Murphy, and Burns.

▲ **Simple crosses mark graves in the Irish Cemetery, Grosse Île. In the typhus outbreak, so many died that bodies were just piled into mass graves.**

Sometimes passengers were moved from their ships and instead quarantined on an **isolated** island. They stayed in these quarantine stations until they were proven healthy.

Quarantine stations prevented serious outbreaks of disease in the cities, but they did little to help those immigrants who were infected. Sometimes, in the unclean conditions of the stations, diseases spread to those who were not sick upon arrival. People called the quarantine stations "fever sheds." For many thousands of Irish, the fever sheds were the only glimpse of North America they ever had. They died there, impoverished and among strangers in a foreign land.

For those Irish who survived the quarantine or were considered healthy upon arrival, the first impression of their new home was exciting and overwhelming. Tall buildings crowded around them and unlike Ireland, there was little open space of green grass to be seen.

▼ **Irish immigrants landing in New York in the 1870s disembarked to find themselves in the middle of a noisy, fast-moving city.**

Eyewitness to History

MRS. JOHN DONNELLY was born in 1861 in Balley Matz, Ireland. Her parents emigrated to the United States when she was still a girl. Here, she recalls what life was like on their farmstead in Nebraska.

" The country was all open prairie. Our nearest neighbor lived one-and-a-half miles distant. We had built a **sod house** and broke a small patch of land with our oxen and planted corn and garden stuff. We had plenty of rain and everything grew. We got corn and lots of vegetables. We made a cellar and stored our vegetables in it for the winter.

We usually had corn bread on our table. Prairie chickens were plentiful. They provided us with meat. Of course the men had to go out and shoot them. But there were so many that they always got some.

In the winter we burned corn stalks, tumbling weeds, and **ox chips** to keep warm. Later on we always had some coal in the winter.

At first there was no school in the neighborhood. After a few years, we built a small school building. We had three months of school during the year. Reading, writing, arithmetic, and geography was taught. Most of the pupils learned to read, write, and figure enough to get them through the world at that time. We didn't need much of the foolishness taught in schools nowadays.

We were Catholics. At first we had no services. Later when a missionary came to Sutton, we went to church there. The trip was not fast, because our oxen took their time. "

Where Irish Settled

The first Irish immigrants in North America, like many other Europeans, settled in British colonies along the east coast. As these colonies grew, land became more crowded and expensive.

Before the 1800s, Irish immigrants to North America often moved to the countryside. Some worked in the fur trade, trapping and exploring, but most settled in rural farms and villages. They cleared the land of trees, built homes, and planted fields. Many others worked in coastal areas as fishers, on ships, and as dockworkers. So many Irish fishers settled in Newfoundland, that the island was called Talamh an Eisc in the Irish language.

In the 1800s, Irish immigrants to Canada continued to settle the countryside, where they became successful farmers and loggers. In the United States, immigrants tended to stay in the large eastern cities where they landed.

Men found work as general laborers in factories and construction. Women also went to factories, or became seamstresses and servants. Even children sold newpapers to earn money for their families.

▲ Many Irish women worked in cotton mills. Some had experience of working in Ireland's linen industry.

Irish Navvies

Teams of Irish laborers helped build many of North America's canals, railroads, sewers, dams, and other large construction projects. They were called "navvies," from the word "navigators," which was an old name for canal-builders in Britain. The navvies often lived in temporary camps near the construction sites with their families. Large camps included quarters or cabins, a school and hospital, stores, offices, and a canteen. After several months or years, construction was finished, and the town was **dismantled**. Most navvies moved on to the next worksite. Some navvy villages, however, grew to become permanent settlements. Irish navvies helped build the Erie Canal in New York, the Welland Canal in St.Catharines, Ontario, and the Canadian Pacific Railway.

The Irish earned such low wages that most could only afford to live in city slums. The terrible conditions in the cities soon led some Irish to leave for the wide-open farmland of Texas and the Midwest. Irish immigrants also settled in Savannah, Georgia where they worked on the canals and railways in the 1830s. In New Orleans, they found employment at the New Orleans canal and Banking Company. By the mid-1800s, Irish settlers were helping each other gain employment and were opening their own companies.

▼ During the 1800s, many Irish prospectors hoped to make their fortunes at California gold mines.

It took a few generations before many of the hardworking Irish families who remained in the eastern cities earned success. Brave Irish factory workers, especially women, fought for and won better wages and working conditions. Irish colleges were built to train doctors, lawyers, and other professionals. Many Irish men found work in the police and fire departments of large cities such as New York and Chicago.

◄ Irish-born men were recruited as soldiers. They fought in the American Civil War (1861–1865).

Eyewitness to History

ROALDUS RICHMOND was born just outside Dublin in the late 1800s. His family moved to New York shortly afterwards, and later on to Boston. Like his father before him, Roaldus became a hardworking stonecutter in the granite "sheds." Here, he remembers his Irish heritage, and talks about his hopes for his own son.

" When we left Ireland I was a baby. My folks had some hard times there, and my father never spoke of Ireland. But my mother was always talking about the blue mountains and the lakes, and she never stopped loving it. She was always singing Irish songs around the house.

My boy wants to take up **aviation** now. My wife don't like the idea, but I think you'd better let a boy do what he wants to do. And flying is getting bigger all the time. If he wants to fly, and he can get into it, I won't try to stop him. It never came into his head to be a stonecutter like his father and grandfather. I'm glad he don't want to cut stone. Not that I'm ashamed of my trade. I'm proud of it.

But for my boy I want something better, you know, the way any man does for his son. That's why I don't mind the hard work. I'd work harder and longer if it'd mean more money coming. Our shed is pretty cold and damp in the wintertime. The floor is dirt and the wind blows through the walls... If it wasn't for my family I might start hitting the bottle like some of the boys do, and let everything slide. But they keep me going all right, and I'll work as long as I can. I don't want my boy to have to work like this all his life. "

Anti-Irish Prejudice

In addition to the day-to-day hazards of life on the frontier or in the city, some Irish suffered prejudice in their new homes after immigrating.

▲ **In the mid-1800s, Irish laborers were often made fun of in newspaper cartoons. They were shown with baboon-like faces.**

I rish Roman Catholics in particular were the target of unfair treatment in both the United States and Canada. Life was some what easier in regions such as Québec, where there were large numbers of French Catholic settlers. Elsewhere, Irish Catholics were shunned, mainly because of their religion but also because so many were poor.

Most people who first settled the British colonies in North America held strong Protestant beliefs. Many, including Irish Protestants, had been peasants in Europe, but others had some wealth and skills that gave them status and power in their new land. Protestants ran the governments, cities, and almost all businesses and institutions such as schools and charities.

Before the mid-1800s, some Irish Roman Catholics had settled in North America, but more came in after the Famine.

"Know-Nothings"

In the United States in the 1850s, prejudice against Irish Catholic and German immigrants led many people to meet privately to plot against them. When asked about their secret meetings, these people replied that they knew nothing. Soon this movement formed its own political party, called the American Party, or "Know-Nothings." Many Know-Nothing politicians were elected on their promises to keep immigrants from voting, or even coming to America at all. The party lasted only a few years, but the prejudice behind it remained, especially in the east. This was one reason many Irish moved west.

Protestants grew afraid of their numbers, particularly in the United States. They put forward many reasons for mistrusting their Irish Catholic countrymen. Many believed Catholics were more loyal to the Pope than to their adopted land. Newspapers, magazines, and other media in New York, Boston, and other cities portrayed them as dirty and ragged, lazy, or alcoholic and violent.

Prejudice against Irish Catholics often prevented them from finding good jobs. Employers avoided hiring them, and wrote "No Irish Need Apply" when they advertised for workers. The Irish were forced to accept jobs for lower pay, and then other workers blamed the Irish for putting them out of work. Eventually, bad feelings against Irish Catholics, which sometimes spread to Irish Protestants, led to anti-Irish marches, strikes, and riots.

The Irish were determined to build lives for themselves in North America. They set up their own community groups, churches, and schools. Irish workers fought for better wages at work and encouraged new Irish-owned businesses by combining their savings to offer loans. Eventually Irish politicians won seats in government. By the 1900s the Irish were a respected part of their communities.

▲ Many Irish immigrants lived in slums, such as New York's Donovan Lane tenement buildings.

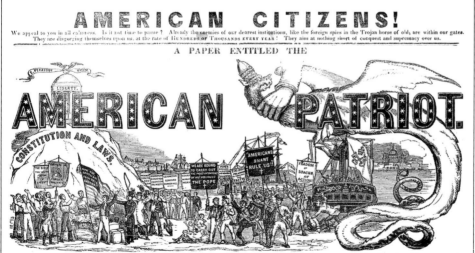

◄ Irish Catholics faced terrible prejudice. This advertisement for an anti-Catholic newspaper shows Irish immigrants just arrived from Cork. These include priests, a drunken mother, and many ragged children.

Religion and its Traditions

The Irish brought their religious traditions with them to North America. They built many churches and established respected schools, clubs, and institutions.

Irish churches have helped set up community hospitals and charities throughout North America, as well as many important Catholic schools and colleges. The Christian Brothers of Ireland established the Manhattan College in New York, La Salle University in Philadelphia, and Saint Mary's in California. In the United States, the most famous school is Notre Dame University in Indiana, which was founded in 1842.

Many of the traditions of North America's Irish communities are based around their Roman Catholic and Protestant beliefs. One religious holiday that has become the largest celebration of Irish **culture** in the world is St. Patrick's Day.

St. Patrick's Day celebrations were brought by immigrants to North America in the 1700s. Each year, it is marked in many towns and cities with parades and parties. New York City holds the largest and most enthusiastic parade in North America, with bands of pipes and drums, dancing, and flags. One of the favorite traditions in many parades is the "wearing of the green."

▲ **This St. Patrick's Day card features many green shamrocks and a traditional Irish harp.**

▼ **In Chicago, the river is colored green for the celebration of St. Patrick's Day.**

For the wearing of the green, people dress up in green clothes and wear Irish shamrocks. Green is the color associated with Ireland and Irish Catholics.

St. Patrick's Day celebrations were traditionally organized by Irish social clubs. These clubs, which often did charity work for Irish immigrants and their children, were formed by local church communities. Many such Irish social clubs are still active today.

After the 1850s, St. Patrick's Day parades became popular in towns and cities across the continent. They were a chance for the growing communities of Irish Catholics to proudly show off their accomplishments and influence in North America. Today, Irish and non-Irish alike, come together to enjoy the parades.

◄ Irish Catholic priests crossed the Atlantic to work as missionaries. Father Constantine Scollen arrived in 1862 and worked in Canada and the United States for 40 years.

Orange Lodges

In Canada, many Irish Protestants united in the early 1800s to form Orange Lodges. These organizations, based on similar ones in Great Britain, were created in honor of the Protestant king, William III of Britain, whose nickname was "William of Orange." William defeated the Catholic king James II at the Battle of the Boyne (1690) in Ireland.

Members of the Lodges promoted Protestant pride by pitting themselves against Irish Catholic immigrants. As decades passed, they became less prejudiced. Lodges are still strongly Protestant, but today they focus on working to make their communities better.

▶ Members of the Royal Orange Lodge of Calgary, Alberta meet in 1916.

Music, Dance, and Literature

Irish immigrants brought with them a wealth of culture including traditional Irish music and song, dance, poetry, and folktales.

Irish music was one of the strongest traditions brought by the immigrants. Today, both traditional and modern Irish music is loved for its sad, haunting melodies and brisk, happy beats. Musicians play such instruments as the Irish harp, the *uilleann* bagpipes, the *bodhran* goatskin drum, the *flageolet or* tin whistle, and the fiddle.

Irish musicians originally came from all over Ireland's countryside and at first played only their own local styles. In North American cities, they heard other Irish styles for the first time. Irish-inspired music later reached millions of people through Irish Americans, such as musical-comedy composer George M. Cohan and actor-singers "Bing" Crosby and Gene Kelly. In Canada, the Irish traditional fiddle music of the Atlantic provinces, and western Canada is well known all over the world.

▲ Competitors at a *feis* or Irish dancing competition, wear traditional embroidered costumes.

◄ Irish music and dance was often the only form of evening entertainment for Irish American laborers in isolated lumber camps.

The Irish Language

Irish, or Gaelic, was once spoken throughout Ireland. Over centuries of English rule, Irish became a language spoken only in the isolated countryside. When these rural people moved to North America, they were encouraged to speak English. Today, Irish has been **revived** by many people in Ireland and is spoken by a few in the United States and Canada. Some Irish words were adopted into the English language.

English	Irish	English	Irish
bog	*bogach* ("soft")	shanty	*sean tigh* ("old house")
galore	*go léor* ("plenty")	slew	*slúag* ("a large number")
keen	*caoinim* ("lament")	slogan	*sluagh-ghairm* ("army cry")
shamrock	*seamróg* ("clover")	whiskey	*uisce beathadh* ("water of life")

Irish dance, performed to traditional music, is popular throughout North America. Skilled dancers compete at traditional dance competitions, called *feis*.

There are three common kinds of Irish dance. Jigs are brisk and dancers hop, slide, and skip to the music. Reels can be very fast and exciting, and female dancers must do plenty of leaping. The hornpipe is much slower and is performed in hard shoes that click like tap shoes. The audience judges the performers on how they bring fresh ideas to the famous set music, which includes pieces called *The Blackbird*, *Garden of Daisies*, *The Three Sea Captains*, and *King of the Fairies*.

Some people say that the sad and joyous themes of Irish music can also be read in the poetry and literature of their descendants. Many writers have drawn upon their Irish roots in their work. Eugene O'Neill is the most famous Irish American writer, and he became the first U.S. playwright to win the Nobel Prize for Literature, in 1936. His later plays, including *The Iceman Cometh* and *Long Day's Journey Into Night*, drew upon his family's Irish immigrant history.

Other acclaimed Irish American writers include Mary McCarthy, whose autobiography *Memoirs of a Catholic Girlhood* was published in 1957, and F. Scott Fitzgerald. Fitzgerald's novels were mostly about the glamor and destructive behavior of rich young people during the 1920s.

▼ F. Scott Fitzgerald's most famous novel was *The Great Gatsby* (1925). Francis Ford Coppola made the story into a movie in 1974.

Here to Stay

The Irish and their descendants have played important roles in the United States and Canada. They were among the continent's first settlers and leaders. Since those early days, they have built powerful industries, fought wars, led governments, and entertained the world.

There are many North American politicians with Irish roots. One of the earliest and most famous American presidents, Andrew Jackson, elected in 1828, was the son of Irish immigrants. The first Roman Catholic of Irish descent to run for president was Alfred Smith in the 1920s, but it was not until John F. Kennedy was sworn in that a Catholic held the post. Former prime minister Brian Mulroney is among Canada's leaders of Irish descent.

Many Irish descendants became popular heroes. Irish heroes fought for workers' rights, such as fair wages and safer working conditions. Mary Harris Jones, better known as "Mother Jones," pushed the labor movement in the United States. She traveled across the country fighting for child labor policies and strong labor unions. Union leader George Meany was the grandson of Famine emigrants. He was elected president of the American Federation of Labor by 1952.

Many Irish descendants have become great business leaders. Henry Ford built one of the first cars, the Model-T Ford. His use of the **assembly line** revolutionized manufacturing around the world. Businessman Alexander T. Stewart invented the department store. Canada's famous chain of "Eaton's" department stores was founded by Irish immigrant Timothy Eaton, who had learned his trade in Ulster, Ireland.

▲ In 1961 John F. Kennedy became the first Roman Catholic of Irish descent to become U.S. President.

◄ Nellie L. McClung fought tirelessly for people's rights. Her efforts helped bring the vote to women in Canada in 1918.

Angela's Ashes...

Best-selling author Frank McCourt, an Irish-American, was born in Brooklyn, New York to Irish immigrant parents. His family returned to Limerick, Ireland when he was a child. Frank survived the hardships of living in poverty, by developing an interest in stories. He returned to the United States at the age of nineteen. Frank became a high school teacher in New York City and later, an author. In his memoir *Angela's Ashes* (1996), he tells of his family's struggles growing up in the poor slums of Limerick. In 1999, a movie was made based on his book *Angela's Ashes*, in which Frank was the narrator.

The fields of arts and entertainment have produced many Irish stars. One of the earliest and greatest film stars, Buster Keaton, was famous for his comedic silent films. He was also part of a family routine known as the Three Keatons. Canadian actor Hume Cronyn is one of Canada's most respected stage and film actors. Artist Georgia O'Keeffe became a celebrated twentieth century artist. She began painting at age twelve and became famous for her flower paintings.

I AM COMING

▲ **Buffalo Bill Cody traveled the U.S. and Europe with his shows.**

Irish sports stars have included the bare-knuckle boxer John L. Sullivan and baseball's Michael J. "King" Kelly. Kelly, was a catcher and he was the first one to use signs to call a pitch.

▶ **Leading lady Grace Kelly starred in many wonderful movies of the 1950s, including *High Noon*, *Rear Window*, and *High Society*.**

Glossary

ancestor A family member from the past, such as a grandparent.

assembly line Manufacturing where each worker concentrates on producing a single part.

aviation Flying.

Britain United country of England, Scotland (1707), Wales (1536), Northern Ireland (1800).

Christianity The religion of those who follow the teachings of Jesus Christ and the Bible.

colonies Land settled or conquered by a distant state.

consigned Handed over.

convert To change from one religion to another.

corrupt Acting badly, for example by taking bribes.

culture A group of people's way of life, including their language, beliefs, and art.

denomination An organized religious group within one faith.

descendant A family member, such as a child, or grandchild.

dismantled Taken down.

embark To board a vehicle.

emigrate To leave one's country for another country.

epidemic A time when disease affects many people in one area.

famine A serious lack of food in a country or area.

feat An amazing action.

freight ship A ship intended to carry goods, not passengers.

heritage The language, beliefs, lifestyles, and art that people receive from past generations.

immigrant Someone who comes to settle in one country from another country.

importunate Urgent.

indentured servant A person who works as a servant in exchange for their travel expenses and keep.

isolated Far away from people.

listless Lacking in any energy.

logging Cutting trees.

malnourishment Poorly fed.

medieval European history between 400 A.D., and 1350.

missionary Religious person who works to change people's religious beliefs.

ox chips Dung, burned as fuel

pestilence Infectious disease.

plantation Land on which crops are grown using cheap labor.

Pope The head of the Roman Catholic Church.

preceding Going before.

prejudice An unfair opinion.

prospecting Looking for minerals underground.

Protestant A Christian whose faith and practice differs from the Roman Catholic Church.

quarantine Being kept away from other people so that infectious diseases do not spread.

revived Brought back to life.

Roman Catholic A Christian who follows the teachings of the Roman Catholic Church.

sepulcher A tomb.

shamrock A plant like a clover with leaves divided into three.

sod house A home made of turf.

trapping Setting traps for animals, usually for their fur.

wan Pale or sickly.

Index

1 2 3 4 5 6 7 8 9 0 Printed in the USA 5 4 3 2 1